This little book
belongs to

_____

BABY'S FISHING FOR A DREAM,
FISHING NEAR AND FAR,
HIS LINE A SILVER MOONBEAM IS,
HIS BAIT A SILVER STAR.

··· ALICE C.D. RILEY ···

The Baby Book

by
Mary Engelbreit

Andrews and McMeel
A Universal Press Syndicate Company
Kansas City

10 9 8 7 6 5 4 3 2

ISBN: 0-8362-4602-0

Library of Congress Catalog Card Number: 91-78256

...IT IS NOT A SLIGHT THING
WHEN THEY, WHO ARE SO
FRESH FROM GOD,
LOVE US.

-DICKENS-

The Baby Book

A new little one
in your world
means excitement…

...patience

S O C I A T E · © ME 83

. . . love

A BABE IN A HOUSE IS A WELL-SPRING OF PLEASURE, A MESSENGER OF PEACE AND LOVE, A RESTING-PLACE FOR INNOCENCE ON EARTH; A LINK BETWEEN ANGELS AND MEN.

M.F. TUPPER

...laughter

· Manners ·
A child should always say what's
true
and speak when he is spoken to,
and behave mannerly at
table,
at least as far as he is able.

· FOR KAREL ·

. . . magic

. . . memories

OLD MOTHER GOOSE,
WHEN SHE WANTED
TO WANDER,
WOULD RIDE THROUGH
THE AIR ON A
VERY FINE GANDER.

. . . innocence

...fun

. . . a link with the past

...and a beautiful promise
of tomorrow.

THE LAP of LUXURY